How to Plan and Implement a Peer Coaching Program

Pam Robbins

Association for Supervision and Curriculum Development
Alexandria, Virginia

The Author

PAM ROBBINS is an internationally recognized consultant in training, research, and organization development (21 N. Newport Dr., Napa, CA 94559).

ΛSCD®

Association for Supervision and Curriculum Development
1703 N. Beauregard St. • Alexandria, VA 22311-1714 USA
Telephone: 1-800-933-2723 or 703-578-9600 • Fax: 703-575-5400
Web site: http://www.ascd.org • E-mail: member@ascd.org

ASCD publications present a variety of viewpoints. The views expressed or implied in this book should not be interpreted as official positions of the Association.

Printed in the United States of America by Automated Graphics Systems.

ASCD members: $6.95
Nonmembers: $8.95
ASCD Stock No.: 611-9114S
ISBN: 0-87120-184-4

Library of Congress Cataloging-in-Publication Data

Robbins, Pamela.
  How to plan and implement a peer coaching program / Pam Robbins.
    p.   cm.
  Includes bibliographical references (p.   ).
  ISBN 0-87120-184-4: $6.95
    1. Teaching teams—United States.   2. Mentors in education–United States.   3. Action research in education–United States.   I. Title
  LB1029.T4R63   1991
  371.1'48—dc20   91-27082R
                                                              CIP

08   07   06   05   04   03   10   9   8   7   6

How to Plan and Implement a Peer Coaching Program

Acknowledgments

Many thanks are due to Linda Gaidimas, Rose Kauffman, Sue Salny, Karen Steinbrink, Charles Tinman, and Pat Wolfe, whose content suggestions were invaluable. Thanks are also due to Michael Krauss, who caused me to reflect and learn, and to Darlene Evans for her clerical assistance and encouragement. Finally, special thanks to David Caro, whose insights, friendship, support, and humor serve as a continuing source of inspiration for my thoughts and creativity.

Introduction

T eachers often feel alone in schools. Although they may interact with hundreds of individuals each day, teachers rarely observe others in the act of teaching or work collaboratively. In many buildings, norms exist that run counter to the theme of collegiality. The issues of how educators are treated and how they work within their own schools need to be resolved if we are to have lasting, significant change in schools. We need to build bridges across classrooms and restructure our schools in ways that capitalize on the talent that exists in individual classrooms. Teachers need to have opportunities to open classroom doors, talk together about teaching and learning, and solve problems.

> [The] theory of professional empowerment is that when given collective responsibility to make educational decisions in an information-rich environment, educators will work harder and smarter on behalf of their clients: students and their parents (Glickman 1990).

Peer coaching offers one way to bridge the gap imposed by isolation. It can become an avenue to develop a collaborative workplace where staff members interact freely to address curriculum and instruction, observe and teach each other, develop and analyze materials, plan, and solve problems together. The outcomes of such endeavors are marked by enhanced student performance; dedicated, energized professionals; and a stimulating workplace. The opportunity to observe and participate in work with colleagues becomes so revered that staff members work hard to support and nurture the many structures that promote this collaboration.

This book examines one structure of collaborative work in schools: peer coaching. Although this book specifically addresses peer coaching as a process involving teachers, at some schools, administrators have also been invited to participate in peer coaching activities. In the pages that follow, peer coaching is defined; a spectrum of peer coaching activities is discussed; specific observation, data-collection, and conferencing strategies are outlined; and guidelines for designing a site-based peer coaching program are offered. Contextual variables that influence the success of peer coaching efforts are explained, and strategies are presented for maintaining the momentum of coaching efforts. A personal planning guide is offered to help readers identify appropriate next steps, and the Appendix includes a listing of helpful ASCD resources for coaching and references.

1.
A Definition of
Peer Coaching

Summary and Suggestions

This chapter defines peer coaching and addresses the objection that often surfaces in reaction to the word coach. *Various types of peer coaching activities are discussed, and three approaches to peer coaching are explained.*

If you are using this chapter as part of a workshop, after presenting the definition, consider asking participants to respond to the following question: "In the best of all possible worlds, what would you want peer coaching to look like, sound like, and feel like at your site?" Record participants' responses and then ask participants to brainstorm what they would like to call their program. Examining desired outcomes and naming the program serve to build ownership and commitment.

Peer coaching is a confidential process through which two or more professional colleagues work together to reflect on current practices; expand, refine, and build new skills; share ideas; teach one another; conduct classroom research; or solve problems in the workplace. Although peer coaching seems to be the most prominent label for this type of activity, a variety of other names are used in schools: peer support, consulting colleagues, peer sharing,

1

and caring. These other names seem to have evolved, in some cases, out of teacher discomfort with the term *coaching*. Some claim the word *coaching* implies that one person in the collaborative relationship has a different status. This discomfort is to be expected because the label may imply to some an inequality among colleagues that is inconsistent with the historical norm of a nonhierarchical structure within the teaching ranks. As research and experience inform us, "The reality is that a teacher has the same 'rank' in his or her last year of teaching as the first" (Sizer 1985). Teachers have the same classroom space, number of students, and requirements. Regardless of how coaching relationships are labeled, they all focus on the collaborative development, refinement, and sharing of craft knowledge.

Peer coaching has nothing to do with evaluation. It is not intended as a remedial activity or strategy to "fix" teachers. Several school systems have supported peer coaching as a way to increase feedback about instruction and curriculum. One teacher, reflecting on the support that peer coaching offers before the formal evaluation process, described it as "a dress rehearsal before the final performance." Another spoke of peer coaching as "a time when you can take risks and try out new ideas, instructional strategies, or different approaches to the curriculum and discuss the results with a trusted colleague."

Types of Peer Coaching

Peer coaching is as individual and unique as the people who engage in it. Some peer coaching involves two or more colleagues working together around the shared observation of teaching. In this instance, there is generally a pre-conference, an observation, and a post-conference.

The teacher who invites a coach in, referred to as "the inviting teacher," steers the coaching process. The inviting teacher identifies the focus of the observation, the form of data collection, guidelines for the coach's behavior in the classroom during the observation, the parameters of the discussion of observed teaching, and the date and time of the observation. This approach will be discussed in detail in Chapter 4.

Other types of peer coaching might involve a pair or a team of teachers co-planning a lesson or curriculum unit. Still other types might involve problem solving, videotape analysis, or study groups. Some coaching may occur between an expert and a novice or between experienced and less-experienced teachers.

Shulman (1991) suggests still another approach in which teachers share stories about teaching experiences. This approach conceptualizes teaching as a narrative act and provides a nonthreatening way for teachers to share pedagogical knowledge. For example, within a small group of teachers, one teacher discussed how she explained to students why certain elements on the periodic table are called *noble elements*. The metaphor she related to students suggested that noble people have everything they need; therefore, students should remember that noble elements don't need anything, either. Another teacher recalled a story of how nobility tend not to mix with other social groups. Noble elements, accordingly, don't mix with other elements. By sharing stories in this way, teachers increase their technical repertoire within a "safe" context—teachers feel safe because the activity in which they collaboratively engage is storytelling and cannot be confused with advice giving, an activity shunned in many school cultures.

Other teachers have used the peer coaching process to conduct action research. In this situation, a teacher formulates a set of hypotheses about classroom practices and develops a plan to test them by asking a colleague to observe and take notes. Later, the colleagues discuss and analyze the data. Some teachers have kept reflective journals of their findings over time.

An additional form of out-of-classroom coaching is called "Talk Walking" (Caro 1991). This strategy is designed to help teachers engage in (1) collegial dialogue focused on instructional and curricular issues and (2) physical exercise, an element frequently missing from the teacher's work day. When Talk Walking is used in a workshop, it can help teachers integrate new learnings with existing classroom practices.

After a workshop segment has been completed, teachers are asked to reflect on how they might use the content they have just learned back on site. They then pair up and go outdoors for a walk, during which they discuss their reflections about the applicability of the training to their own classrooms.

Talk Walking can also be used in the schools, independent of a workshop. In this setting, teachers arrange a time to meet for a walk during which they might discuss plans for a specific lesson, reflect upon a unit that has been taught, talk about specific students, or share recent reflections or learnings related to curriculum and instruction.

Collegial dialogue of this nature has both cognitive and physical implications for teacher growth. It also fosters the development of trust among colleagues committed to sharing craft knowledge and serves to create professional norms of experimentation while encouraging teachers to learn from one another. In the all too busy day of a teacher's life, Talk Walking brings exercise and fresh air—two important elements for teaching and thinking—into the daily routine.

The forms peer coaching can take are limitless. It might focus on instructional strategies, curriculum content, classroom management practices, specific students, particular problems, or instructional skills such as questioning techniques or process skills to generate higher-order thinking. These activities might occur within the classroom or in the teachers' lounge or workroom. Two individuals, a trio, or a team might work together in peer coaching arrangements. Figure 1.1 shows a variety of the forms peer coaching can take. These may be formal arrangements and involve a structured pre- and post-conference focused around an observation, or informal arrangements such as a storytelling session.

In peer coaching, the focus is on the teacher as learner. Fullan, Bennett, and Rolheiser-Bennett (1990) describe four aspects of the teacher as learner—the technical, the reflective, the research, and the collaborative—which are played out in a variety of coaching experiences. They suggest:

4

Figure 1.1
Forms of Peer Coaching Activities

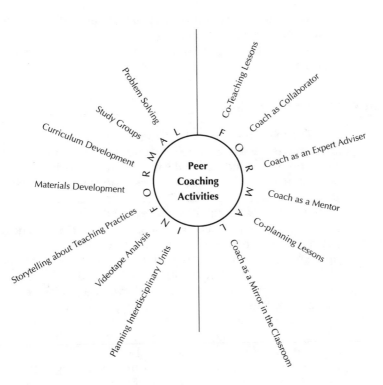

The mastery of a technical repertoire increases instructional certainty; reflective practice enhances clarity, meaning and coherence; research fosters investigation and exploration; collaboration enables one to receive and give ideas and assistance. Each aspect has its separate tradition of research and practice.

These aspects should be integrated and offer a useful framework for conceptualizing a variety of coaching activities that have at their core the notion of the teacher as learner.

Approaches to Peer Coaching

There are a variety of approaches to peer coaching. One type is designed to help teachers transfer into classroom practice new skills they have learned in a workshop or training session. This type of coaching usually follows training in specific strategies or methods. For instance, if the training has addressed the elements of a lesson strategy such as concept attainment, the coaching process would revolve around how the teacher is implementing that strategy in the classroom. Teachers pair with consultants or one another so that feedback can be given about the application of the new strategy in the classroom. The focus of peer coaching activities in this context is directly related to the workshop or training content. Research has shown that this approach promotes skill transfer (Joyce and Showers 1980).

However, if this is the only form of coaching that teachers experience, the process may become routine and the coaching may turn into coaching as unreflective practice (Hargreaves 1989), wherein teachers simply go through the motions of labeling the implemented behaviors and consequences. When this happens, the aspects of the lesson about which the teacher is genuinely curious may go unaddressed (Robbins 1984). To be effective and sustained over time, coaching activities must have a deliberate focus. And the focus must be one that matters to the individuals involved.

Other approaches to peer coaching involve colleagues working collaboratively around issues unrelated to a specific focus generated by shared training. This type of peer coaching relies on a teacher-specified focus. Here the approach is intended to increase professional sharing, to refine teaching practices, and to enhance teacher reflection. It may also include conducting action research, solving problems related to instruction or curriculum design and delivery, or resolving problems with specific students.

Regardless of the type or approach, peer coaching efforts all share a collaborative quest to refine, expand, and enhance knowledge about the teaching profession. These approaches make learning about the business of teaching accessible to all teachers in the workplace. While coaching activities may involve only segments of a school staff, collectively they can increase the climate of collegiality *if they become an integral part of life at the school and if the school culture provides a hospitable environment.* But this is not always the case. Ironically, some of the same factors that provide a rationale for coaching cause coaching attempts to be stifled or fail. Chapter 2 addresses this irony.

2.
The Case for Peer Coaching

Summary and Suggestions

This chapter begins with two scenarios that allude to the rationale for peer coaching. It then goes on to examine this rationale, which consists of seven reasons. These include the need to:

- *Reduce isolation among teachers*
- *Build collaborative norms to enable teachers to give and receive ideas and assistance*
- *Create a forum for addressing instructional problems*
- *Share successful practices*
- *Transfer training from the workshop to the workplace*
- *Promote the teacher as researcher*
- *Encourage reflective practice*

If you are using this guide to plan a workshop, you should present the rationale for peer coaching immediately after the definition. You might use the following scenarios to introduce the rationale and ask participants to compare their own experiences with the seven reasons for coaching. As adult learners, participants need to understand the purpose of peer coaching and see how their own experiences relate before they become involved.

A Scenario

Carol Briggs, Teacher
Douglas County Schools, Castle Rock, Colorado

It used to be that we came to school and propped open the large fire doors of our classrooms. The teachers in our building would visit back and forth, sharing personal and professional conversations as we prepared for the day's instruction. Then one day, the fire marshal came and removed the fixed doorstops that we used to prop open the doors. The stops were condemned because they didn't meet fire code standards. I remember how I felt when the door slammed shut. It was like the final wedge had been driven between me and my colleagues. As I reflected on this experience, it seemed strange that a small comfort we had all taken for granted—a little doorstop—could be removed with such great consequences. When the door slammed shut, our collegial dialogue diminished.

A Scenario

Xan taught for 33 years in the Vacaville (Calif.) Unified School District. When she announced her retirement, the teachers at her school honored her with a party. When the party was over and the party planners cleaned up, they reflected on how Xan had touched their lives as teachers. One teacher said, "Whenever I had students who had difficulty with the concept of borrowing in math, I sent them to Xan and, miraculously, they came back understanding how to borrow." Another teacher smiled and commented, "I sent students to her, too—with the same results!" A third teacher inquired, "How did Xan teach these students?" All three teachers stopped and looked at one another, as they realized that Xan had left that evening and taken her secret with her.

And so it is that teachers often leave their mark on students but not on the teaching profession. It wasn't that Xan didn't want to share; it was simply that the school where she taught had no avenues for developing a shared knowledge base about teaching. Teachers went about the business of teaching in a congenial way. But the talk in the teachers' lounge was about good restaurants, social events, and sports—not about teaching practices and their consequences. Thus, as in many schools, much of the expertise in individual classrooms remained well-kept secrets to the rest of the staff.

These scenarios about teachers are familiar. Most schools have limited avenues for collegial work. The very structure of the physical plant, busy classrooms, and bureaucratic schedules seem to impede the quantity and quality of dialogue among colleagues. However, in some settings, teachers have gone to extraordinary lengths to ensure that collegial work develops and prospers. In these schools, collegial structures such as peer coaching are in place, and information about successful instructional practices flows from one teacher to the next, advancing the prospects for student success. Settings characterized by such collegial practices require a supportive context, achieved as a consequence of careful planning; financial, personal, and organizational commitment; and individual dedication. These settings tend to be the exception, however, not the rule. Why is this the case? The history of the teaching profession offers a possible explanation and also helps us to understand the rationale for peer coaching.

The Rationale for Peer Coaching

Teaching is rooted in a tradition of isolation. From the original one-room schoolhouse to current structures, described by some researchers as "one-room schoolhouses repeated every few yards down the corridor" (Glickman 1990), the physical characteristics of schools impose barriers to communication about successful instructional and curricular practices. As a result, many well-kept secrets exist in individual classrooms, and year after year, teachers leave their mark on students' educational experiences but not a trace on the teaching profession. Despite hundreds of years of collective expertise in individual schools, few avenues exist for teachers to tap this expertise.

One argument in the case for peer coaching is that it offers a way to break the isolation and tap the craft knowledge of others. But this requires that teachers relate to one another in a collegial way, sharing their knowledge about teaching across classrooms. Many teachers have never experienced this type of interaction.

Frequently, the historical tradition of isolation produces unwritten laws or norms that govern relationships among colleagues in schools. Because of this, it is generally not the norm for teachers to observe one another. A "live and let live" protocol prevails in many schools. Advice giving is often perceived as an unwelcome practice or as bragging. As a consequence of these norms, many teachers feel to ask for assistance is a sign of incompetence (Rosenholtz 1989). They feel uncomfortable about venturing into another teacher's classroom or having another teacher visit theirs. The norms governing collegial interactions in schools stand in stark contrast to those of the medical and law professions, where joint work and collegial consultations are the norm.

Peer coaching, properly implemented, can transform the norms of isolation into norms of collaboration. A second reason for coaching is that, when teachers work together regularly to reflect on, analyze, and refine teaching practices, and when they find this work intrinsically meaningful, collaborative norms develop in the workplace. In the best of circumstances, "greater contact among teachers can be expected to advance the prospects for student success" (Little 1989) as well as revitalize the workplace. In a culture characterized by collaborative norms, teachers are empowered to take action together and make wise choices related to instruction, curriculum, and student learning. These norms become central to teachers' daily lives.

Another explanation for the tradition of isolation is related to the nature of teachers' work. One researcher suggests that with the expanded curriculum of the '90s, teachers not only teach but perform a variety of other roles such as counselor, health consultant, and nutritionist. Many teachers feel that their isolation affords them the only way to plan and perform the work required to fulfill their professional roles (Flinders 1988).

A third benefit of peer coaching is that it helps teachers work smarter, not harder. Many teachers who have participated in peer coaching comment that learning from one another often helps in dealing with the multitude of demands on the teacher's role and saves time, too. One teacher said:

> If I can learn from a colleague, I can save time by not having to reinvent the wheel. I used to spend hours working alone, planning after school. Now a group of us meet regularly and address issues of concern. We're finding that by integrating the curriculum, we can teach more content within a shorter amount of time. What a relief that discovery provided!

Peer coaching provides teachers with a way to address their instructional problems.

Still another reason for isolation is related to teacher choice. Many entered the profession because of the autonomy the individual classroom offered. These teachers consciously chose the culture or context of isolation and now find themselves bound by norms and traditions that celebrate individual work and accomplishment. Even if a teacher desired to collaborate with another, it would be difficult to change old ways of operating, and little time would be available during the normal duty day for colleagues to meet and discuss practice. Within this existing context of isolation, many teachers wonder, "How do I measure up?" or "Is there another way that I might reach this child?" Because of limited opportunities for collegial interactions, most teachers' on-the-job learnings are primarily achieved through trial-and-error experiences. Properly implemented peer coaching can celebrate individual work and accomplishment, yet simultaneously assist teachers in learning from one another rather than from errors alone. Herein lies the fourth reason for peer coaching.

The opportunity to work with colleagues—whether it be called peer coaching, collegial consultation, or collegial work—offers a viable source of support. It also provides a structure for building a shared knowledge base capable of advancing not only the teaching profession but the educational process that contributes to the collective success of individual students.

A fifth argument for coaching has already been discussed in Chapter 1. That is, when attached to specific training, coaching can help promote the transfer of newly learned skills to the classroom, providing the parties involved value the new practice. As one teacher noted:

> It's easy to get swept up in the daily business of teaching, and while you really intend to implement the new practice, you often put it off. Knowing someone is coming to watch me teach causes me to rehearse what I have learned more frequently. The more I rehearse, the smoother my performance, and the greater the likelihood that I'll use my new learnings on a regular basis.

The sixth benefit of coaching is that it provides an avenue for teachers to tailor a staff development plan for themselves. They can become action researchers in their own classrooms and investigate the connections between their own planning and teaching behaviors and the consequences. Teachers can, in this way, modify their own practices as a result of a careful analysis of data a colleague has collected.

The seventh and final reason for coaching is that it can provide a needed window of time for teacher reflection. Research and practice suggest that teaching involves a constant stream of decisions (Jackson 1968) made before, during, and after teaching (Berliner 1984). With this rapid-paced reality of classroom life, teachers rarely have time to reflect. Yet reflection time is precisely what teachers need to gain new insights about teaching and learning that can help refine current practices. Peer coaching provides not only the time to reflect but also the opportunity for colleagues to discuss those reflections.

Collectively, the seven reasons for peer coaching appear even stronger when we examine the testimonials of professionals who have become involved and have overcome the obstacles imposed by norms of isolation, bureaucratic schedules, and the fear of teaching publicly. They report the following benefits:

- An improved sense of professional skill
- An enhanced ability to analyze their own lessons
- A better understanding of teaching and learning
- A wider repertoire of instructional strategies
- An increased sense of efficacy
- Stronger professional ties with colleagues
- Improved teaching performance
- Enhanced student progress
- A better articulated curriculum
- A more cohesive school culture
- A positive school climate

Herein lies the case for peer coaching. What better way is there to invest in and use the knowledge of the school's one natural resource—its teachers?

3.
Before You Jump In

Summary and Suggestions

This chapter addresses both the virtues and the fragility of coaching. The suggested guidelines address issues to consider before jumping into a peer coaching program.

Individuals planning workshops might develop a "lecturette" containing the information in this chapter. Encourage participants to brainstorm questions they have about peer coaching at this point and then address those questions. Building readiness by providing information is a critical part of creating a foundation for a peer coaching program.

So far, peer coaching sounds great! It promises to reduce teachers' isolation, to create a collegial and professional environment in the school, to provide a forum for problem solving, and to promote the transfer of skills from training sessions to the workplace. Peer coaching interactions have the potential to enable teachers to learn from and with one another and to reflect on crucial aspects of curriculum and instruction. However, Little (1985a, 1985b) cautions:

> They also place teachers' self-esteem and professional respect on the line, because they expose how teachers teach, how they think about teaching, and how they plan for teaching to the scrutiny of peers. The challenge becomes how to devote close, even fierce, attention to teaching while preserving the integrity of teachers.

Peer coaching is a delicate process. Because of this reality, great danger is associated with rushing into it. Individuals who might be interested in participating will nonetheless often feel reticent about doing so until they are more comfortable with the concept of coaching and can see what it might offer them. Principals and other school leaders will need to assess the implications of beginning a program. To help launch a peer coaching program, the following guidelines might be useful.

Guidelines for Peer Coaching

• *Examine all the facts about peer coaching, and then compare them with your site characteristics before you determine whether peer coaching is right for you.* Ask yourself why you really want peer coaching. Recognize that planning, implementing, and maintaining a program require a great deal of effort and time.

• *Identify what peer coaching is and isn't.* Because most teachers' only experience in having another adult in the classroom has been in an evaluative capacity, clarify the following seven points before coaching begins.

1. Peer coaching has nothing to do with evaluation. It is observation-based and specific, not general. The coach collects only the specific data that the inviting teacher has requested. The inviting teacher ultimately decides what to do with the data.

2. Peer coaching is based on professional, not social, dialogue. The focus of peer coaching activities is on teaching and its consequences. While a congenial spirit is important for the individuals involved to feel comfortable, the discussion should revolve around professional issues.

3. Interactions should be collegial rather than competitive in nature. Peer coaching activities should be characterized by a stance of equality— we're in this together—rather than a spirit of one-upmanship. The coach should work just as hard in the coaching role as the teacher does in the teaching role.

4. Coaching should be supportive rather than evaluative. The coach's function is to ask questions that encourage the teacher to reflect, analyze, and plan. Even when

a lesson does not go as expected, the coach's role is not an evaluative one. Instead, the coach needs to help the teacher to compare what was expected with what happened and to analyze what might have contributed to the outcomes of the lesson.

5. Interactions between the coach and the inviting teacher should be confidential. Even if the coach observes a fabulous lesson and wants to praise the teacher publicly, he should refrain from doing so. Once the confidentiality of a coaching relationship is broken, it is difficult to rebuild trust. One teacher remarked that even praise delivered privately becomes a burden because it makes her feel she has to be "that good" the next time her partner observes her. And, if the teacher does not ask for praise and the coach offers it after the observation, it is as if the coach has overstepped the boundaries of what the inviting teacher wanted to discuss about the lesson.

6. The focus of coaching visits should change to meet the needs of the inviting teacher. For example, one visit might examine the effects of strategies to promote higher-order thinking skills, and the next visit might focus on the wait time the teacher provides and the student responses elicited.

7. Teachers need to choose whether or not to participate in coaching. The adult learning literature, as well as common sense, suggests that adults have many commitments and demands on their time. Individuals will commit to participating in only those training and related activities that they perceive as realistic, important, and useful. Mandated coaching is rarely effective.

• *Develop a clear understanding of the different forms of peer coaching.* Explain that coaching activities can occur both within and outside the classroom. In the classroom, coaching usually entails a pre-conference, classroom observation and data collection, and a post-conference where data are analyzed. The interactions between the inviting teacher and the coach can be categorized into three types: *mirroring*, where the coach records but does not analyze or interpret classroom action; *collaborative*, where the coach may co-plan a lesson or simply collect data as specified by the teacher and later collaboratively analyze them; and *expert*, where the coach has more expertise or experience with the topic being observed and serves as a consultant to help the teacher learn or refine particular skills. Mentoring fits in this final category as well. These types of classroom interaction should be modeled so that potential peer coaching participants can see what the interactions are like and understand the nonevaluative approach.

Coaching activities outside the classroom can be carried out in a variety of formats, including problem solving, videotape analysis, study groups, materials development, curriculum development, idea sharing, and co-planning of lessons.

• *Provide time for questions and answers.* Teachers will have many concerns when they first learn about peer coaching. They might request additional information and have personal concerns as well as concerns related to how they will manage their teaching responsibilities and find time to coach, too.

• *Solicit teacher input regarding the possible features of a site-based peer coaching program.* Adults come to any learning experience with a wide range of previous experiences, knowledge, skills, self-direction, interests, and competence. Teacher input is critical to ensuring that the peer coaching program is designed to reflect their needs and the characteristics of the site (e.g., budget, schedule, substitute availability).

• *Identify the preconditions for change and the cultural variables that will affect the success or failure of peer coaching at your site.* Peer coaching should not be viewed simply as another innovation but should be designed to become an integral part of school life. This will involve what Fullan (1982) calls a change in the school as an institution that increases its capacity and performance for continuous improvements. Whether this is possible or not depends largely on existing conditions in the workplace. The Mid-continent Regional Educational Laboratory (1983) has identified three preconditions for coaching:

1. A perception of "good, but growing." There must be a general perception on the part of the staff that they are good, but there's always room for growth. The introduction of peer coaching does not mean that what they're currently doing is wrong or needs to be examined.

2. A reasonable level of trust. The teachers and principal involved must have a reasonable level of trust among them. According to Bird (1985):

> There is a way of talking and acting which separates the question of practice and its consequences from the question of people and their competence, and which separates habits from self-esteem. Then, the practices and habits can be put on the table and dissected while the person who uses them remains intact.

3. A sense that people care for one another. A climate must exist in the school that conveys the sense that people care about each other and are willing to help one another. Another variable affecting implementation success is the existing degree of teacher collegiality. Studies by Fullan and Pomfret (1977) and Little (1982) show that teacher collegiality and other elements of collaborative cultures are known to be related to the likelihood of implementation success. Therefore, if a school's culture is already characterized by teacher collegiality and norms that promote collaborative work, peer coaching efforts are more likely to flourish. The degree to which experimentation and risk taking are valued, supported, and rewarded at a school will also affect the potential success of peer coaching.

• *Analyze the support available for peer coaching.* Verbal support alone will not suffice. Both expressive and symbolic support for peer coaching are needed. This includes the provision of time for coaching activities, money for training, development and released time, resources for classroom observations, celebrations to reward what the school culture values, and protection by those in leadership roles from outside interference and competing demands.

The guidelines set forth in this chapter should be considered by a team, not just one individual. They should be discussed in detail, their ramifications should be examined, and then if the context is ready and staff are interested in pursuing coaching, the next step involves creating a planning team to design a program tailored to the characteristics of the implementation site. This process is discussed in detail in Chapters 7 and 9.

4.
The Peer Coaching Process and Logistics

Summary and Suggestions

This chapter provides an overview of the in-classroom coaching process including the pre-conference, observation, and post-conference. It describes the three types of conference structures mentioned in Chapter 3 in further detail: mirroring, collaborative, and expert coaching. Logistical considerations, such as how to facilitate released time for coaching, as well as how coaching pairs are formed, are also addressed.

If you plan to use this chapter as the basis for an inservice, it would be useful to model each conference type and discuss how to use these approaches onsite. Ask participants to identify logistical concerns regarding their own settings.

In-classroom peer coaching involves colleagues working together around the shared observation of teaching. In these instances, there is generally a pre-conference, an observation, and a post-conference. The cognitive coaching approach (Costa and Garmston 1990) offers a useful model for these activities.

The Pre-Conference

At the pre-conference, the teacher who functions as the coach asks the inviting teacher (the teacher who has requested to be coached) to explain the lesson purpose, what led up to the lesson, and what will follow. The coach might also ask about student characteristics and class norms for behavior, as well as any concerns about the lesson or observation. Sometimes, the coach and the inviting teacher might arrange a signal for the teacher to give the coach to leave the room if the lesson is not going as expected. The inviting teacher explains the lesson to be taught and specifies the focus of the observation. However, the coach and the inviting teacher decide together how the data might best be collected. Generally, the focus is something about which the teacher is genuinely curious. It might have an instructional, curricular, or student emphasis. Essentially, it is as if the teacher is a researcher in his own classroom, and the coach is the data collector.

The discussion between colleagues usually includes talk about where the coach should sit or stand to collect data and whether the coach should interact with students. The inviting teacher also determines the parameters of the discussion of the lesson at the post-conference.

The coach's role is to facilitate the inviting teacher's thinking about the lesson to afford a dress rehearsal of the actual teaching performance. This role usually includes asking probing and clarifying questions that serve two purposes. First, they help the teacher to fine-tune thinking about the lesson and, at times, to develop a "fall-back" plan in case the lesson doesn't go as desired. Second, these questions assist the coach by clarifying the desired focus of the observation and by specifying how the data are to be collected. The pre-conference generally concludes with the coach asking for feedback about what she did during the conference to facilitate the teacher's thinking before the lesson. This feedback allows the coach the opportunity to reflect and determine which coaching strategies are helpful so that these can be repeated in future sessions. Asking for feedback in this way also models a spirit of reciprocity. It is as if the coach is committed to working just as seriously in the coaching role as the teacher is in the teaching role. This

The Observation_____

Coaches focus data collection efforts on a variety of topics. Some examples include higher-order thinking skills, teacher-student interaction, student time on task, physical proximity, wait time, use of motivation variables, verbal flow, use of a particular instructional strategy and its effects, active participation, or the effects of a particular curricular approach such as whole language. The inviting teacher determines the particular focus so that he feels in control of the discussion about the observed teaching.

In no way is evaluation a part of the coaching interaction. For example, if the inviting teacher asks the coach to determine if there is appropriate pacing in the lesson, the coach needs to ask, "If pacing is appropriate, what will I see?" This allows the coach to avoid being put in a judgmental role. She then needs to simply record the presence or absence of those behaviors specified by the inviting teacher.

In the early stages of a peer coaching relationship, the inviting teacher often picks a safe focus—one that often will yield positive data. As trust builds between the coach and the teacher, and the two have the opportunity to switch roles, the inviting teacher might be more willing to experiment, take risks, and "let his or her rough edges show" (Little 1981). The teacher and coach soon realize that it is precisely these rough edges that give them something to hang onto as they examine the practice and consequences of teaching. As one teacher put it, as she grew more comfortable with the peer coaching process she realized that "anything worth doing is worth doing poorly at first!"

Coaching should be a dynamic process. The focus of coaching visits will change as the inviting teacher wishes. On one occasion, an inviting teacher asked her coach to record the questions she asked, how many seconds she waited before eliciting student responses, which students responded, and what they said. When the inviting teacher examined her data, she discovered that she consistently called on some students first, while asking others to "elaborate on the answer." Thus, the students routinely called on to elaborate on the answer always had more wait time. For this reason, the inviting teacher decided to be more conscious of which students she called on, and in what order, as she taught. During the next observation, she asked the coach to focus on collecting data about the response patterns so that she could determine whether she met her personal objective of distributing the opportunity for wait time.

Before the observation, the inviting teacher usually tells his class about the coach's visit: "Mr. _____ will be coming in to watch me teach today. At another time, I will be visiting his classroom. At this school, teachers believe in learning from one another." Many teachers have commented that using statements such as these affords them an opportunity to model, at an adult level, the type of cooperative learning they are promoting in their own classrooms among students.

The Post-Conference

Post-conferences are diverse and can be categorized into three types: mirroring, collaborative, and expert. The type used depends on the preference of the inviting teacher and is often influenced by the time available to meet, the trust between the coach and the teacher, and the history of the coaching relationship. The mirroring post-conference takes the least time and might be selected if the teacher does not desire a lot of dialogue about the observation. In the mirroring post-conference, the coach simply says, "Here are the data you asked me to collect. If you have any questions, please let me know." The coach then hands the data from the observation over to the teacher. The coach's role in this example is that of a confidential, objective observer and data collector. The inviting teacher analyzes the data alone.

In a collaborative conference, the conversation usually is characterized by a mutual discussion of the teaching observed. The coach asks the inviting teacher to reflect on what happened as expected or planned and what happened differently. The inviting teacher also analyzes what teaching and student behaviors contributed to the lesson outcomes. Out of this discussion, the teacher determines what changes to make when teaching the lesson again. At the end of the conference, the coach solicits feedback about the coaching strategies employed. Throughout the post-conference, the discussion is guided by the parameters set forth by the inviting teacher in the pre-conference. The inviting teacher decides what to do with the data. Sometimes the coach helps plan the initial lesson in the pre-conference and, in the post-conference, collaboratively analyzes and helps replan the lesson if it is to be taught again. This type of post-conference might take as long as thirty to fifty minutes and involves a much deeper, mutual analysis of the data.

In an expert conference, the expert has more experience or expertise in either a particular grade level or with a particular instructional or curricular technique. In the post-conference, the expert guides the inviting teacher to analyze the lesson, much as the coach does in the collaborative conference. The expert conference differs from the collaborative, however, in that the coach often teaches during the pre- and post-conferences.

For example, one novice teacher asked her coach to analyze the variety of ways that students were asked to actively participate in her lesson. The coach wrote down specific examples of active participation during the lesson observation. At the post- conference, the novice reflected, "I used 'think, pair, share,' choral responses, and signaling, but I wish I could have used additional strategies. Could you share some others with me?" The coach responded to the novice's questions with an inquiry: "What other techniques have you tried in previous lessons?" The novice recalled her use of response cards and individual chalkboards.

In this example, the expert facilitated the novice's reflection and rehearsal of strategies used in the past. This questioning increased the likelihood that the teacher could recall the techniques quickly in the future. The expert's questioning facilitated the novice's recall of past efforts and provided a strategy that the novice could use in the future, even when the expert coach wasn't there. Thus, the post-conference strengthened the teacher's ability to help herself—a vital survival skill in isolated classrooms. If the novice had not been able to recall any techniques used in the past, the expert might have shared some of those she had seen others use and then ask the novice to consider which might best suit the particular lesson and her teaching style.

Even in the expert conference, the inviting teacher has control over what happens and how the data are used. The expert post-conference usually takes thirty minutes to an hour. Trust is a critical factor in the expert conference because some teachers fear that acknowledging an instructional difficulty or asking for assistance might be construed as an open admission of incompetence (Rosenholtz 1989).

The mirroring, collaborative, and expert forms of the post-conference are not a developmental continuum. They represent a range of options for interaction between the inviting teacher and the coach. For example, the inviting teacher might work with an expert coach for one observation to learn more about teaching social skills in cooperative learning. In the next coaching session, the inviting teacher might ask the same coach to collaboratively plan, observe, and discuss a lesson on social skills. The third time they work together, the inviting teacher might ask the coach to function as a mirror and to observe student time on task in a cooperative learning lesson. The collective goal of these coaching sessions is to facilitate the teacher's ability to reflect on and analyze teaching. The teacher plays the role of action researcher in his own classroom. He is assisted by the coach, who serves as a data collector and, in some cases, as a co-investigator.

Another form of pre- and post-conferencing is tied to a specific strategy or curricular approach taught during an inservice session. Here, the purpose of coaching is to facilitate skill transfer from the workshop to the workplace. In this instance, the observation focus is not steered by the inviting teacher; it is linked to the workshop content. Hence, if the workshop addresses the elements of a specific lesson strategy, such as synectics, the coaching process revolves around the classroom implementation of this strategy or innovation.

Besides the formal, in-classroom coaching structures discussed previously, teachers have experimented with a variety of other, out-of-classroom forms of coaching. For example, they have co-planned lessons, cooperatively developed interdisciplinary units, created grade-level cooperative learning materials, analyzed and discussed videotaped teaching episodes, solved problems, met in study groups to discuss topics of interest, and taught one another new instructional and curricular approaches. These efforts all share the element of peer support to refine, expand, and enhance knowledge about the teaching profession. They break down the walls between classrooms to build a rich knowledge bank from which all teachers can draw.

Logistical Considerations

Peer coaching should be a voluntary activity. When it is mandated because it is written into a plan or endorsed by the administration, it runs the risk of becoming what Hargreaves (1989) has appropriately labeled "contrived collegiality," an activity that forces unwanted contacts among unconsenting adults, consuming already scarce time.

How often peer coaching partners meet is a function of need or desire, as well as opportunity, which is often tied to school budget. Many peer coaching partners meet at least twice a month so that each individual can play the role of both inviting teacher and coach. Released time to participate in peer coaching is provided through a variety of means. Often teachers use "prep periods." Others work in trios with teacher A taking over two classes to release teacher B to observe teacher C. Some programs use a librarian so that the coaching teacher's class learns study skills while their teacher is out peer coaching. Still others involve guest lecturers who teach students about a subject related to their course of study. At times, the principal or vice principal will teach a class. Other peer coaching programs use substitute teachers, often referred to as "guest teachers" to enhance their status with students. When substitutes are used, it is useful to provide them with training to help them manage the classrooms. Many schools request the same substitute on the same day each week. Teachers often report worrying about the loss of student contact, even though the gains they report from participating in peer coaching are great.

How should coaching pairs be formed? Coaching needs to occur in a psychologically safe environment. Therefore, teachers should select their own partners. This selection is often based on shared interests, areas of expertise, friendship patterns, geographic proximity, similar teaching styles, a desire to stretch their style, or the grade levels at which they teach. Some teachers purposefully choose partners who have a style similar to theirs; others find it more challenging to select a partner with a different style. For those who work in trios, teacher A observes teacher B, teacher B observes teacher C, and teacher C observes teacher A. In one district, an entire grade-level team worked together. One teacher on the team pre-conferenced with all of the other teachers on the team and then taught the same lesson in each team member's classroom. Finally, the entire team post-conferenced together.

Another teacher recommends, "You should have a rule that peer coaches can get a divorce if the relationship is not working." Peer coaches in some schools change by semester; others remain constant. Who works with whom or for how long should reflect teacher choice. Every teacher should have the opportunity to play both the role of inviting teacher and coach.

In those schools where peer coaching practices have become a way of life, teachers report tremendous benefits. These benefits are so significant that they motivate teachers to continue with coaching activities in spite of budget cutbacks that, in some schools, have eliminated the possibility of using substitute teachers to make time for coaching activities.

5.
Deciding on a Focus and Collecting Data

Summary and Suggestions

This chapter addresses the importance of the inviting teacher selecting a specific focus for the observation and matching this focus with an appropriate data collection instrument. Several such instruments are discussed. In addition, it is recommended that the use of these instruments be negotiated in detail during the pre-conference between the inviting teacher and the coach.

If you plan to use this chapter for a training session, you may find it useful to ask participants to brainstorm possible ways to focus an observation. Record participants' ideas and then have them sketch out observation instruments to reflect each focus on their list.

Teachers report that one of the most difficult aspects of peer coaching, after conquering feelings of discomfort about teaching publicly, is deciding on a focus for the observation. One teacher suggests that this is largely the case because, in most instances, the focus of classroom observations has been steered by the particular evaluation instrument used by the principal or a particular strategy or approach taught in an inservice. Now, all of a sudden, the sky is the limit! Where to start is a real dilemma.

If the peer partners have not worked together for any length of time, the inviting teacher often selects a safe focus—something he is confident about and does well. As trust develops, the focus is generally determined by something the inviting teacher is genuinely curious about. In the early stages of a coaching relationship, it is not uncommon for the inviting teacher to say to the coach, "Just pick anything to focus on." The coach should not be the one to select a focus. Clearly, teachers are more committed to a focus or goal they have formulated rather than one established by someone else. Hence, it is important that the coach respond by asking the inviting teacher to consider what kind of classroom data might be of interest.

Often it is helpful to brainstorm a "menu" of options from which to select when this situation arises. Examples on this menu might include teacher-student interactions, student time on task, verbal flow, teacher proximity, wait time, questioning skills, use of motivation theory, use of reinforcement theory, specific instructional strategies and their effects, curricular approaches, active participation techniques, gender expectations and student achievement, and a particular child or small-group focus. The focus selected should reflect something the teacher feels is both important and perplexing. It should be a variable that in some way affects student learning and is under the teacher's control.

Once the inviting teacher selects a focus, the next step is determining how the data will be collected. It is essential that the inviting teacher and coach talk about the data collection instrument in detail so that the data collected during the observation match the desired focus. Although a variety of commercial instruments are available, many teachers have found that developing their own instruments allows them to tailor data collection to their specific needs.

For instance, if a teacher wishes to focus on teacher proximity, the coach might simply draw a seating chart and use a pencil line to indicate where the teacher walks during a class period. If the teacher also wants to know what students are doing during that time, the teacher and coach could develop a set of codes to represent behavior and identify time intervals when sweeps would be made. In

Figure 5.1, for example, sweeps are made every five minutes, and the teacher asked the coach to collect data about six types of behavior. The figure shows the results of the first sweep. Some coaches might feel that to collect so much information is an overwhelming task. If this is the case, the coach needs to express her concerns to the teacher. She might say, "I want to do the best job I can when I collect data for you. I'm worried about focusing on so many things. If you were to identify a first priority for this observation, what would it be? Could we possibly focus on the second priority during our next coaching session?"

Because there are various ways to collect data for a particular focus, peer coaching partners should discuss options and even sketch them out before selecting one. Otherwise, the coach may assume that the teacher wants the data collected in one way, when in fact the teacher has a completely different idea in mind. In a recent example, an inviting teacher asked her coach to collect data about her use of wait time after questions she had posed. In addition, she wanted the student responses to her questions. After the observations, the coach handed over the data. The format looked like this:

? (3 seconds)	"They are mammals because they share the characteristics of having hair and nourish their young with milk from mammary glands."

The inviting teacher had expected the question to be scripted (written down), a column for wait time, and the students' responses scripted using the following format:

Question Scripted Here	Wait Time in Seconds	Scripted Student Response

The teacher and coach learned from this experience and decided to avoid future misunderstanding by discussing data collection approaches in more detail during the pre-conference. This situation also reveals that cognitive style and modality preferences also affect teachers' preferences for data collection (Gregorc 1985).

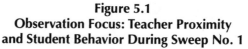

Figure 5.1
Observation Focus: Teacher Proximity
and Student Behavior During Sweep No. 1

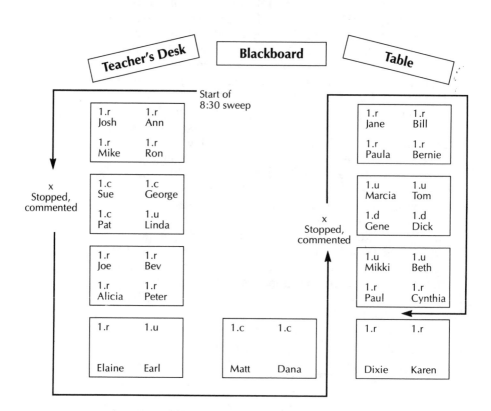

CODE

Sweeps

1 - 8:30
2 - 8:35
3 - 8:40
4 - 8:45
5 - 8:50
6 - 8:55
7 - 9:00
8 - 9:05
9 - 9:10
10 - 9:15

Codes

u - uninvolved
c - chatting
d - disruptive
r - reading
? - asking questions
a - active participation

Figure 5.2
Verbal Flowchart

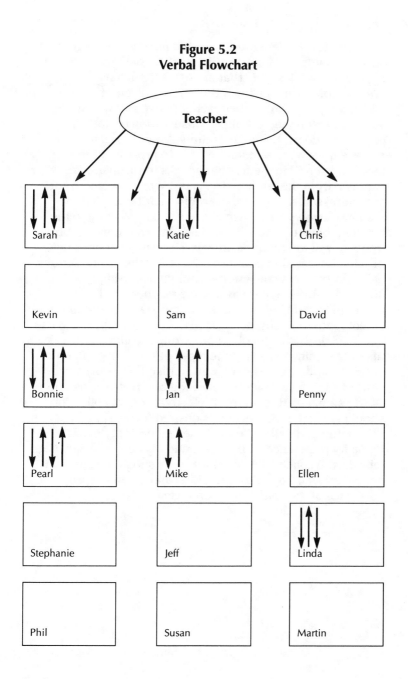

The ASCD videotape series *Another Set of Eyes* contains several examples of observation instruments ranging from simple to complex. One that many teachers have found comfortable to start with is the verbal flowchart (Figure 5.2). It shows to whom the teacher spoke and which students responded during an observation period. To create this chart, the coach simply draws boxes to represent each student and a circle to represent the teacher. Each time the teacher speaks to the class, an arrow is drawn from the circle to the class. When specific students are addressed, arrows are drawn in their boxes. If they respond, arrows are drawn in their boxes pointing to the teacher. While this approach yields information about the frequency of interactions and class coverage, it does not provide information about the quality of these interactions.

Another data collection technique is to simply write down what the teacher says. Some teachers find this technique useful, but it can be difficult. Other teachers have videotaped or audiotaped lessons. While this approach can be useful, it usually involves preparing the class, and it is time-consuming to review the tapes at the post-conference. Teachers and coaches may want to discuss the pros and cons of each data collection method before selecting one.

In summary, the method selected for data collection should (1) match the teacher's desired focus, (2) be negotiated in detail, (3) reflect the teacher's style and modality preferences if possible, and (4) be a manageable task for the coach. Observational data should be specific, not general, and objective, not interpretive. In this way, the outcomes of the conference can be maximized.

6.
Conferencing Strategies

Summary and Suggestions

This chapter identifies skills vital to successful conferencing and effective communication. Six technical and social principles are addressed, as well as a useful stance of curiosity with which to approach the conferencing process.

If you are using this chapter to plan a training session, review the six principles and provide examples of each. Then describe the pre- and post-conferences. Give participants the opportunity to generate questions and practice asking them with feedback from their peers and workshop leader.

> The real voyage of discovery consists not in seeking new lands but in seeing with new eyes.
>
> —Marcel Proust

Perhaps the most critical and delicate component of peer coaching is the conferencing process. Through this process, the inviting teacher is afforded a new look at his classroom. Being observed by a peer is a new experience for many teachers, and functioning as a coach puts them on unfamiliar ground, often causing them to approach the conferencing and observation processes with great hesitancy. For this reason, what is said and how it is said during the interactions in the pre- and post-conferences are crucial.

Little (1985a) describes a helpful stance from which the inviting teacher and coach can approach the discussion of observed teaching. She points out the need for a spirit of "curiosity about teaching and learning," as if the coach and inviting teacher are "unravelling a mystery together, not monitoring each other." It is essential for the coach to look for and describe the teaching practice that the inviting teacher has identified as the focus. But this must be done in a way that does not put the teacher's sense of competence or self-esteem at stake.

Six Principles of Effective Conferencing

Little describes six principles that help in "separating the practice from the person conducting the lesson." Designed for work with teacher advisers in Marin County, California, they are modified here to include work among peer coaches.

Technical Principles

Common language. A common language is helpful to decribe, understand, and refine teaching. However, if a common language (usually based on terms taught during training) does not exist, the coach and teacher can ask one another specific questions to elicit clarity and under-standing of the terminology each individual uses, thus enhancing the quality of dialogue during conferencing. For example, if the teacher uses the term *concept attainment* in referring to a teaching strategy and the coach is not familiar with the term, she might inquire, "What do you mean by *concept attainment*? Could you explain the process to me?" Often, explaining something in common language makes the point clearer to the sender as well as the receiver of the information.

Focus. A specific focus is critical because it narrows the parameters of what is to be observed and discussed. Setting limits in this way can become a comfort for the inviting teacher because it clearly establishes what will be observed and discussed. For the coach, having a focus helps make data collection more concrete and precise because the notes and observation records will be tied tightly to the proposed focus.

Hard evidence. Peer coaching partners use objective data as a basis for generating questions, drawing conclusions, and developing alternative approaches to the lesson. Relying on a record of evidence helps keep coaching objective.

Social Principles

Interaction. Peer coaching partners interact in both the pre- and post-conferences. Conferencing serves as a vehicle for joint work on teaching and conferencing skills and provides an opportunity for teachers to learn from one another.

Predictability. Predictability helps peer coaching partners to build and maintain trust. When the coach collects only the data requested by the inviting teacher, discusses only what the teacher requested, and maintains confidentiality on a regular basis, the inviting teacher soon comes to rely on this predictability. This generates confidence in the coach as well as comfort in the relationship.

Reciprocity. Peer coaching partners "build trust by acknowledging and deferring to one another's knowledge and skill, by talking to each other in ways that preserve individual dignity and by giving their work together a full measure of energy, thought and attention" (Little 1985b). The coach vows to work just as hard at observing and conferencing in the coaching role as the teacher does in the teaching role.

Conferencing Goals

Three goals are generally associated with peer coaching conferencing; these are derived from *cognitive coaching* (Costa and Garmston 1990). They are trust, learning, and autonomy.

Since coaching needs to occur in an environment where individuals feel safe, *trust* is a major component. Trust must be created and maintained between the individuals in the coaching relationship, and they must have trust in the coaching process, trust that interactions will remain confidential, and trust that peer coaching is not a remedial process but one that allows both parties the opportunity to grow and learn from one another.

Learning comes as a result of interactions during the pre- and post-conferences. Both the coach and the inviting teacher are engaged in reflection, inquiry, analysis, and synthesis. Both learn about teaching and conferencing.

As teachers engage in peer coaching, they become more *autonomous*. They become so used to the pattern of questions the coach uses to get them to reflect on and analyze the lesson that in the coach's absence, they can ask these questions of themselves. Hence, teachers develop the ability to reflect, self-analyze, and self-prescribe.

Conferencing Approaches

Cognitive coaching (Costa and Garmston 1990) offers a useful approach to conferencing, which includes the pre-conference, the observation, and the post-conference.

The Pre-Conference

The pre-conference is designed to provide an opportunity for the inviting teacher to "unpack" her thinking about the lesson to be taught. The coach asks questions that afford the teacher an opportunity to reflect on her plans for the lesson before teaching it. Sometimes the teacher expresses concern about a particular part of the lesson, and the teacher and coach might collaboratively devise a fall-back plan. The pre-conference also gives the coach an opportunity to ask the inviting teacher to clarify the lesson objective, purpose, desired student behaviors, and the lesson context (review, introduction to a unit, practice, new or old material, what preceded, what will follow, etc.). In addition, the inviting teacher identifies a desired focus for the observation and specifies how she wishes the data to be collected. Often a sample data collection instrument is developed.

The coach's role is also clarified. This involves describing where the coach is to sit or stand while collecting data and whether the coach is to interact with students. A signal is usually arranged that the inviting teacher may use if she wants the coach to leave at any time during the lesson.

At the conclusion of the pre-conference, the coach summarizes his understanding of the lesson and observation task. The inviting teacher provides feedback as to the accuracy of the coach's understanding and clarifies misinterpretations as necessary. Then they decide when the observation and post-conference will take place.

The pre-conference usually takes ten to thirty minutes, and it, as well as the post-conference, should be conducted in a place where both teacher and coach feel comfortable. For a summary of the goals of the pre-conference, see Figure 6.1.

Many teachers learning conferencing skills indicate that the most difficult aspect of the process is determining which questions to ask. This is true because there is no recipe for questions. Rather, questions need to be generated by the coach in response to the inviting teacher's answers to previous questions. (See Figure 6.2 for an example of this process.) To develop fluency, however, it is useful to practice formulating a variety of questions based on the goals of the pre-conference.

Figure 6.1
The Pre-Conference

The goals of the pre-conference are to:
- Build trust and rapport
- Promote rehearsal and reflection
- Gather information about the lesson objective(s)
- Elicit information about the purpose of the lesson
- Collect information about teacher and student behaviors
- Review the lesson context
- Anticipate teacher concerns
- Determine the role of the observer
- Clarify the focus of the observation
- Decide how data will be collected
- Summarize their understanding of the lesson and data collection process
- Identify the time of the observation and post-conference

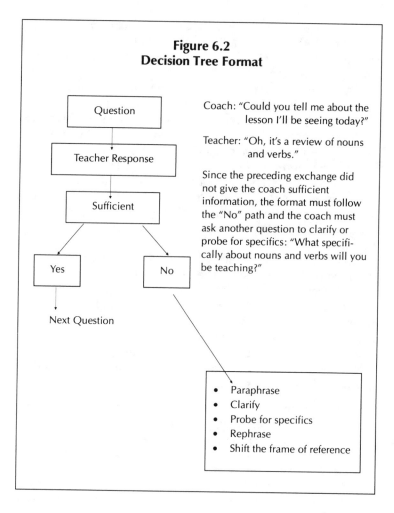

Figure 6.2
Decision Tree Format

Question

Teacher Response

Sufficient

Yes

No

Next Question

Coach: "Could you tell me about the lesson I'll be seeing today?"

Teacher: "Oh, it's a review of nouns and verbs."

Since the preceding exchange did not give the coach sufficient information, the format must follow the "No" path and the coach must ask another question to clarify or probe for specifics: "What specifically about nouns and verbs will you be teaching?"

- Paraphrase
- Clarify
- Probe for specifics
- Rephrase
- Shift the frame of reference

The Observation

During the observation, the peer coach, using the agreed upon format, collects only the data that have been requested. The observation usually takes thirty to fifty minutes. Sometimes the coach makes a copy of the observation data and gives it to the inviting teacher to study before the post-conference.

The Post-Conference

The post-conference usually begins with an open-ended question to elicit the teacher's feelings or thoughts about the lesson—for example, "How do you feel the lesson went?" After the teacher responds, the coach asks him to reflect on the lesson to uncover the source of these feelings. The teacher's conclusions are often compared with the coach's observations and discussed.

The overall goal is for the coach to ask the inviting teacher questions to promote reflection about the lesson, as well as an analysis of what happened as expected and what happened differently. In addition, the teacher is asked to project, if he were to teach the lesson again, what he would replicate and what he would do differently. This approach is more of a discrepancy analysis. It shifts the focus from one that might be painful if a lesson didn't go as intended to one characterized by a problem-solving spirit. Throughout the process, the coach asks questions and presents observational data as appropriate. In many models, the coach employs feedback and labels, such as "You did _____ . That was an example of an anticipatory set. It was effective because _____ ." The peer coaching model, however, requires the teacher to reflect on the lesson and analyze it. In this way, the teacher, not the coach, gets to rehearse cause-effect relationships between teaching behaviors and student outcomes. This allows the teacher to reconstruct a lesson and analyze its effects and later infer how it will contribute to the knowledge base that he will use to plan future lessons.

The post-conference usually concludes with the coach asking for specific feedback about her use of conferencing strategies. This allows the coach to further develop conferencing skills and models the reciprocity mentioned earlier, which contributes to trust. The data the coach has collected are handed over to the teacher at the end of the post-conference.

Again, the goals listed for the post-conference may be used to create questions as a practice activity to develop fluency. For a summary of post-conference goals, see Figure 6.3.

Figure 6.3
The Post-Conference

The goals of the post-conference are to:

1. Promote teacher reflection on the lesson by
   - Recalling teacher and student behaviors
   - Comparing actual and desired behaviors
   - Analyzing why behaviors were or were not performed
   - Making inferences about achievement of lesson purpose and objective

2. Generate future plans

3. Provide feedback about practices for both teacher and coach

4. Build motivation to participate in future peer coaching sessions

The coach gives the written data to the inviting teacher.
The inviting teacher ultimately decides what to do with the data.

Communication Skills

Several communication skills are employed throughout the conferencing process. These include the use of:

- *Silence* or *wait time*, which give the partners time to reflect and think
- *Paraphrasing* or *active listening* to check for understanding
- *Clarifying* to make information easier to understand
- *Pressing for specificity* to elicit more precise information and details
- *Avoiding negative presuppositions* to eliminate negative messages embedded in language (e.g., Can you think of another way you might have taught this lesson?)
- *Reframing* or shifting the reference point or context
- *Neutral comments*, which help generate rapport

Teachers who have used these skills and the cognitive coaching conferencing strategies in both the inviting teacher and coaching roles report that they think more comprehensively about their teaching before, during, and after instruction. They also note that the conferencing process enables them to process information using higher-order thinking skills—a practice they are working to instill in students. Conferencing in this way also creates bonds between teachers, adding to the degree of teacher collegiality in the school. This variable, as illustrated in Chapter 7, is vital to the ongoing peer coaching program's success.

7.
Contextual Factors Affecting the Success of Peer Coaching

Summary and Suggestions

This chapter introduces eleven organizational and four individual contextual factors to consider when designing a peer coaching program.

If you plan to use this chapter as part of a workshop, ask participants to think of their own school contexts and brainstorm those factors that would support peer coaching and those that would hinder it. Consider and discuss how these factors would affect their initial planning efforts.

P eer coaching usually involves pairs, trios, or small groups of teachers working together. In this regard, those participating represent only a segment of the total school culture. However, research has demonstrated (Seller and Hannay 1988, Little 1981) that the success of peer coaching programs depends on the schools providing a hospitable environment. Therefore, it is essential that program planners understand those critical factors that can have a major effect on program design, implementation, and maintenance.

Georgea Mohlman Sparks-Langer (Sparks 1983) provides a useful way of conceptualizing the relationships among these contextual variables, program goals and content, and the school's approach to designing a peer coaching program. This three-nested model suggests that before a planning team can determine the approach to a peer coaching program, it must consider contextual variables.

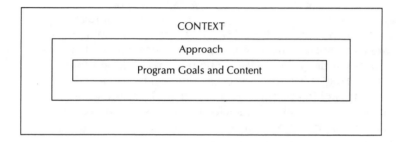

Organizational Contextual Factors _____

As you think about your school, consider the following contextual factors related to the organization.

1. *What is the pre-existing climate of collegiality?* Where working together represents "the way we do business around here" to most teachers, collaboration has become the norm. Little (1989) suggests variations in the form and content of collegiality. Form involves the degree of interdependence as well as the type of collaborative relationship. These types can be ranked along an independence-to-interdependence continuum:

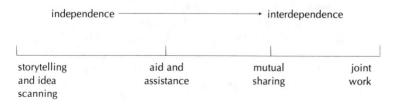

Little claims the first three items on the continuum represent weak ties of collegiality, and with each shift to the right, the "warrant for autonomy shifts from the individual to collective judgment and preference" (1989, p. 5). Experiences need to be provided so that peer coaching relationships and interactions can evolve to the joint-work stage. Otherwise, coaching experiences may run the risk of being relatively superficial, safe, fixed, and inconsequential in terms of their effect on school culture. Recognize that this transition takes time, patience, and support.

2. *Are there norms supporting risk taking and experimentation?* The school culture must encourage teachers to take risks and try new approaches. Whenever we learn something new, our performance usually becomes poorer initially before it gets better. If risk taking is not supported at a school, teachers will feel uncomfortable about teaching publicly. Risk taking and experimentation provide important avenues for refining practice. As one teacher said, "The opportunity to examine the rough edges of my lessons with a colleague helps me to grow. I learn more from my mistakes than from my flawless performances. If this is the spirit with which I embrace teaching, I can be a lifelong learner, and teaching publicly is no longer a threat."

Risk taking and experimentation need to be modeled throughout the school. For example, the principal could borrow a class and ask to be coached. Feedback about faculty meetings could be solicited. Norms should be examined within departments, the school, the central office, and the community to determine whether they support risk taking and experimentation.

3. *Has the supervisory experience been a pleasant or unpleasant one for teachers?* While peer coaching has nothing to do with evaluation, teachers' previous experiences with teaching in front of another adult—usually an evaluator—will affect their feelings about teaching in front of a colleague. Their opinions also will be influenced by whether the supervisory and evaluation processes have had a growth orientation or a monitoring function to ensure adherence to behavioral standards. If a comfort level does not exist for in-classroom coaching, teachers initially should pursue opportunities to work together outside of the classroom. This will help develop trust, a mutual regard for the other's expertise, and a forum for problem solving.

4. *What is the school's track record regarding staff development?* If a bandwagon mentality has prevailed, the history of staff development might read, "Last year it was cooperative learning; this year it's whole language; next year we'll focus on higher-order thinking skills." And there's probably a slogan around suggesting, "If you wait long enough, this, too, will pass." Peer coaching needs to become an integral part of the school context, not just an innovation for the year. When it becomes a part of the institution, it provides a flexible mechanism for accomplishing a variety of functions: building and refining teaching practices, solving problems, developing curriculums, and planning instruction. When peer coaching is introduced to a staff, this orientation needs to be kept in mind and modeled.

5. *What are the core values of the school?* What do members of the school culture think is important? Is rugged individualism prized, or is value placed on working together, sharing ideas, and supporting one another? Think about the stories teachers tell. What do they celebrate? Listen to the conversations in the teachers' lounge, halls, and the parking lot. What is their focus? How and on what is time spent in faculty meetings? Who chooses the topics for inservice? What do celebrations at school acknowledge? Peer coaching thrives in cultures that revere and respect lifelong learning, creativity, and working together for improved teaching and learning. Identifying the values at your school and determining how they came to be will help you decide if they will support a peer coaching program or if they need to be transformed.

6. *Does leadership support peer coaching?* The Rand study of educational innovations (Berman and McLaughlin 1978) concluded that the major factor affecting the success of the programs studied was administrative support—from both principals and superintendents. Lieberman and Miller (1981) and Stallings and Mohlman (1981) also noted the key role of the principal. It is important to determine whether the school's leadership gives both verbal and symbolic support for peer coaching. Symbolic support includes modeling, providing prime time for discussing peer coaching and related activities, celebrating peer coaching accomplishments or collaborative work, and allocating

funds for peer coaching. Leadership should be viewed as all school leaders, including informal leaders within the culture (Deal and Kennedy 1982) and decision-making teams, as well as the principal and central office staff. Without the support of school and district leaders, the prognosis for the implementation of peer coaching over time is poor.

7. *What else is going on?* Time is a precious resource in schools. A major consideration in determining whether peer coaching might become a way of life in a school is to examine what it must compete with in terms of time, focus, and resources. The simultaneous implementation of other interventions will reduce the energy available to devote to peer coaching. Planning, implementing, and sustaining a peer coaching program is a complex process. It has a human as well as a financial cost attached to it. It will affect several groups within a school: students, teachers, administrators, and support staff. It will also affect the central office and the parental community. Looking for ways to integrate peer coaching with other efforts, such as restructuring, will help conserve precious resources.

8. *Will the bureaucratic structure of the school support peer coaching activities?* Peer coaching activities take time. The bureaucratic structure dictates when people can get together for shared work. Hence, schedule is inextricably tied to opportunity for collegial interactions. Examining to what extent the bureaucratic structure at your school will promote or inhibit collegial relations will help you to determine if it needs to be modified.

9. *What are the existing structures of collaboration at the school?* If staff members have a history of working together, peer coaching will not represent a major departure from the norm. In some schools, collaboration occurs regularly in such forms as grade-level teams, school advisory councils, adviser-advisee programs, veteran-intern programs, and team teaching. It is accepted as a way of life.

Hargreaves (cited in Fullan 1990, p. 15) presents a useful typology for considering the forms of collaboration in school cultures:

fragmented individualism	Balkanization assistance	contrived collegiality	collaborative culture

At the far left is the traditional isolation depicted in Chapter 2. "Balkanization" refers to separate subgroups, which often possess their own internal cultures. Contrived collegiality can "proliferate unwanted contacts among teachers that consume already scarce time with little to show for it." Truly collaborative cultures are "deep, personal, and enduring." They are perceived as central to teachers' daily lives. In truly collaborative cultures, colleagues come together to share expertise; develop knowledge; reflect; and plan for instruction, curriculum, and student learning. This is the "home" peer coaching activities need. Peer coaching activities can also play an integral role in transforming structures of collaboration in the school. If they are perceived as meaningful, collaboration tends to increase.

10. *What is the nature of decision making in the school?* Truly collaborative cultures use a structure of shared decision making. It is important to examine what kinds of decisions are shared and what the rules are regarding how decisions are made. When organizational members have productive experiences collaborating in this way, norms that support collegiality are strengthened. When teachers are involved in decision making, they feel a sense of ownership. Whether to develop a peer coaching program should be a shared decision.

11. *How flexible is the school culture?* It is important to examine how readily new ideas are incorporated in the school to determine the prospects for peer coaching success. It also should be determined whether or not the school culture supports a "one right way" mentality. Peer coaching can be used for a number of functions. In this sense, there is no one right way—peer coaching is very flexible. It can be used as an individual staff development tool, as a skill transfer tool, and for problem solving, program development, and other related teacher empowerment and school improvement purposes.

The school culture should also be flexible enough to allow teachers to become involved in coaching at any time. There will always be some early starters, some folks who want to wait until after the initial rush, and others who are reluctant to participate at all. There should be tolerance and respect for all members of the school and their beliefs. Otherwise, an "in group" and "out group" may develop, which tends to drain energy from the collaborative effort.

Individual Contextual Factors

As you think about individual staff members, consider the following RFIT (Relevance, Feasibility, Involvement, Trust) framework, adapted from Laraine Roberts's work at the California School Leadership Academy (Roberts et al. 1987).

1. *How relevant is the concept of peer coaching to an individual staff member?* If teachers see a connection between their lives as teachers and peer coaching activities, they will be more likely to participate. Several factors will influence their attitudes, including their student-teaching experiences, their first teaching years, school norms, and their own sense of self-confidence and competence.

2. *Is it feasible for the individual to participate?* Feasibility addresses considerations of time—whether the individual believes she can make the time to become involved in peer coaching—and philosophy—whether peer coaching is consistent with the individual's beliefs about how teachers should operate. The latter will affect the teacher's perceptions of norms regarding how teachers should relate to one another, what their responsibilities are, and what type of staff development is important.

3. *Has the individual been involved in deciding whether or not to participate in peer coaching?* Adult learners need a sense of control over what happens to them. Involvement in decision making will clarify what peer coaching is and have a positive effect on their sense of ownership of the program.

4. *What is the degree of trust among individuals at the school and those promoting peer coaching?* Trust is one of the most fundamental variables in peer coaching relationships. If trust exists, teachers will be more willing to teach in front of each other and observe their colleagues. In addition, teachers must trust in the good intentions of those promoting the peer coaching program. Otherwise, it will run the risk of becoming just another structure of contrived collegiality.

The consideration and assessment of these organizational and individual contextual factors will help to determine a school's degree of readiness for peer coaching, the timeline for implementation, and how key individuals can become involved. This is an essential component of the initial stages of program planning, which Chapter 9 addresses.

8.
The Principal's Role in Peer Coaching

Summary and Suggestions

This chapter provides an overview of the roles the principal might play with respect to peer coaching: coach, inviting teacher, coordinator, facilitator/supporter, and champion. The benefits of peer coaching, as they relate to the principal's leadership role, are discussed.

The content of this chapter could be used as background information for administrators who have concerns or questions about peer coaching.

Principals play a vital role in determining the success or failure of peer coaching efforts. They provide both symbolic and expressive support for peer coaching. Symbolically, principals can show philosophical support for peer coaching by modeling the peer coaching process; substituting for teachers while they coach their peers; functioning as a coach or inviting teacher (if asked to do so); allocating time and other resources for coaching; promoting schoolwide norms, such as risk taking, that reinforce the spirit of coaching; creating line item budget allocations for coaching activities; and reserving "prime time" on faculty meeting agendas for discussing coaching practices and experiences.

Principals can also talk about the importance of peer coaching to parents, students, board members, staff, and central office personnel in order to promote understanding and support for the program.

Role Options

The roles that principals might play include coach, inviting teacher, program coordinator, program supporter, facilitator, or program champion. When the principal functions in a coaching role, it is usually the result of an invitation from a teacher who feels comfortable with having the principal as a coach. The principal might also coach a vice principal or another principal who requests feedback on, for example, the way she conducts a faculty meeting.

In a teaching role, the principal might ask to borrow a class in order to teach a lesson. Another teacher might be asked to function as a coach for the principal. This allows the principal to model what he is promoting. It adds credibility to coaching activities and provides the principal with important insights about the demands of coaching activities.

As a program coordinator, a principal might arrange coaching schedules (if the teachers who are involved request this) and substitutes. In addition, she might facilitate the formation of peer partnerships for coaching on a request basis. The coordinator at many sites also duplicates needed materials such as articles and observation forms, arranges for videotaping or audiotaping, and attends to any other tasks necessary to manage the peer coaching program.

Principals can function as supporters or facilitators for coaching programs. In this capacity, they could locate and present research or practitioner articles about coaching and give them to teachers; serve as mini-inservice provider or as coach for the coach (to give the teacher in the coaching role feedback about his behaviors); or act as a facilitator for a discussion, problem-solving, or study group.

Finally, the principal might play the role of program champion. This role requires that the principal lead or promote cultural celebrations to focus individuals' attention within the organization on the importance of peer coaching activities. A champion also protects individuals engaged in peer coaching from outside interference. Still another function might have a public relations emphasis to promote understanding and support for coaching among special interest groups: parents, board members, students, and staff.

Why Would a Principal Want Peer Coaching in a School?

For principals and staff interested in building a collaborative culture, peer coaching offers a process through which teachers can be empowered to take on new leadership roles within the school. Enhanced collaboration among teachers can promote a better articulated curriculum, increased opportunities for interdisciplinary curriculum planning, and a chance to tap the well-kept secrets of practice or "craft knowledge" stored in individual classrooms. This type of collaboration has the potential to promote several positive student outcomes. Teachers benefit by feeling less isolated and having a greater support system of multiple resources for instruction and curriculum as well as for problem solving. Teachers will often teach one another because of this collaborative structure; hence, their practice will be formed less by trial and error. Teachers will build a shared knowledge base about teaching and learning and develop new norms that support experimentation and risk taking.

Peer coaching offers the principal a way to differentiate the supervisory process (Glatthorn 1984) and to extend the amount of feedback available to teachers by creating a structure, in addition to standard supervision, for teachers to view their own classrooms from another teacher's perspective.

All of these activities serve to focus attention on the quality of teaching and the process of professional growth. In this respect, peer coaching offers an opportunity to build a community of learners (Barth 1990) committed to lifelong learning within the schools.

9.
Planning a Peer Coaching Program and Maintaining Momentum

Summary and Suggestions

This chapter addresses three phases of the change process as frames for planning a peer coaching program: mobilization, implementation, and institutionalization. Specific activities are recommended for each stage.

If you plan to use this chapter for training, have participants develop a plan based on the three phases for their own site, designating a facilitator and including a timeline for implementation and benchmark indicators of progress.

Studies of effective change efforts suggest that organizations that successfully institutionalize an innovation move through three phases: mobilization, implementation, and institutionalization (Berman and McLaughlin 1978). These phases provide a useful framework for program planning.

Mobilization

During the mobilization phase, these guidelines will help you conduct readiness activities, create awareness, build commitment, and plan your school's peer coaching program.

1. *Form a planning committee.* To generate broad-based support for peer coaching, invite any interested staff members to serve on this committee. Be sure that individuals who have informal power in the school are represented. It is helpful to have union representation as well. The planning committee's major role is to research peer coaching literature and programs in place, including making site visits; assess the context in which peer coaching will be implemented; develop a program plan to share with the entire staff; and devise program activities once the staff has adopted the plan.

2. *Provide information about peer coaching.* Present the definition of peer coaching, explain how it has nothing to do with evaluation, and share the rationale for coaching. Provide information about peer coaching programs in place, invite teachers from other schools who have implemented peer coaching to speak with the staff, and distribute articles about peer coaching. (These may be used as a jigsaw activity in a staff meeting.) Arrange visits to peer coaching sites so that peer partner interactions can be shadowed and later discussed. Show the ASCD videotape *Opening Doors.*

Many schools hold peer coaching orientations where the agenda is structured around the teachers' questions about the program. If you choose this approach, hold the meeting in a comfortable setting, during prime time rather than at the end of a duty day, and provide refreshments. Give staff members concrete examples of how peer coaching can work.

3. *Emphasize the flexibility of coaching.* Explain in-classroom models for peer coaching (mirroring, collaborative, and expert) as well as outside activities (problem solving, curriculum development, lesson planning, videotape analysis). Provide concrete examples and model them. Tell stories to illustrate your points.

For example, one group of resource teachers were new to peer coaching, so they didn't want to observe one another. Instead, they each created a case study of a problem with which they were wrestling. They met in triads and problem solved with one another. At each meeting, they proposed interventions for one another. They tried these interventions in their classrooms and reported back at the next meeting. This process went on for several months. Their trust in one another grew during these collegial interactions, and gradually these teachers felt comfortable enough to observe one another in the classroom.

Talk about the opportunity to become an action researcher in the classroom, and pursue an investigation that is personally meaningful. Discuss different structures for peer coaching: pairs, triads, teams. Brainstorm options for selecting partners: by discipline, by grade level, or across grade levels and departments.

4. *Develop a vision and a purpose.* Sound program planning must emanate from a clear understanding by all members of an organization of what they want the program ultimately to look like, sound like, and feel like. With this vision in place, program goals and activities will follow logically. Benchmarks of progress should be identified to assess progress toward desired outcomes and allow staff members to relate their daily activities to the larger vision of the program. To create a vision, staff members should be asked to collaboratively describe what the ideal peer coaching program would be like, considering how it would affect the school, classroom, teachers, students, administrators, and parents. Besides guiding program activities, this vision-building process will build motivation and commitment, as well as reinforce the notion that peer coaching will be an ongoing, integral part of the school. Core values will surface.

5. *Examine the issue of time.* Since time is a critical resource for coaching, it is important to identify what vehicles exist to provide time. For instance, if a school has common planning periods, that time might be used for coaching activities. If time is not readily available for training and coaching activities within the school context, a special task force should study the issue and recommend how time might be made available.

6. *Identify sources of support and resources.* The availability of human and financial support as well as material resources will dramatically affect the scope of the implementation effort. If, for example, there is little money for released time to conduct coaching, or a limited pool of substitute teachers, other avenues, such as one teacher

covering two classes, will have to be pursued. This might produce an energy drain and inhibit the rate of implementation. Participation that involves hardship may lower the prospects of program success.

7. *Go slowly.* Build support and understanding. Take time to create trust. Think big, but start small. Create early opportunities for success. And give teachers ownership of the program so that the coaching effort becomes of, by, and for teachers.

8. *Identify an on-site facilitator.* This person will help make the coaching program run smoothly by arranging for released time and taking charge of technical details, such as finding space for meetings and making sure ready-made observation instruments are available. This makes it easier for teachers to participate in peer coaching.

9. *Identify individual concerns and address them accordingly.* One useful framework for determining what kind of information school people need when they are first introduced to an innovation is the Concerns-Based Adoption Model (Hall and Hord 1987). CBAM can help program planners identify awareness, informational, personal, management, consequential, collaborative, and refocusing concerns and respond to them accordingly.

10. *Plan how the program will be institutionalized.* Planning for institutionalization is often neglected in the mobilization phase. Thinking about how you want peer coaching to look when it is an integral part of your school can shed light on important implementation activities you should conduct to help reach that goal.

Implementation

Once readiness is achieved and planning activities developed, you are ready for implementation.

1. *Provide training in peer coaching.* Training sessions should include theory, demonstration, practice, and feedback, as well as time to reflect and plan. Training should be *voluntary.* It is useful to space training sessions over several weeks so that teachers have the opportunity to try out new practices. Figure 9.1 provides examples of training topics addressed over time.

Figure 9.1
Overview of Peer Coaching Training Sessions

Session 1   Overview of the research on peer coaching:

                                A context for peer coaching
- collaborative goal structures in schools
- peer coaching, school norms, and culture
- social and technical principles of coaching
- organizing for peer coaching

                                Exemplary peer coaching models
- in classrooms
- outside classrooms

Session 2   Overview of observation instruments for peer coaching:
- interaction analysis
- time off task
- script taping
- checklists
- verbal flow
- homemade versions

Session 3   Factors influencing peer coaching relationships:
- how we look
- what we value

                                A model of factors influencing teacher thinking and behavior:
- modality preferences
- educational beliefs
- mind style
- learning styles

Sessions 4 and 5   Advanced conferencing skills
- the pre-conference
- the post-conference

Session 6   Fine-tuning communication skills
- mediational questions
- probing for specificity
- identifying and staying aware of presuppositions

Session 7   Change theory and effective staff development practices
- what the research says
- implications for peer coaching
- planning for maintenance

Before holding pre- and post-conferences in classrooms, peer coaches have found it useful to schedule ten-minute lessons for pre- and post-conferencing practice in a safe, training-room environment. This usually involves groups of six teachers: One teacher teaches three adult students, and the remaining two teachers function as coach and coach's coach. The roles rotate so that each teacher experiences every role. The teachers should allocate time to discuss this role-playing experience.

2. *Provide a variety of follow-up support services.* Plan both formal and informal ways for teachers to receive feedback about their efforts to implement training in the workplace. This should include coaching the coaches as they initially practice this role.

3. *Provide training in memory research and factors that affect thinking and behavior.* These two training topics are usually of interest to teachers whether or not they plan to become involved in peer coaching. They provide an avenue for a shared training experience for staff; offer skills that can be immediately applied in the classroom with students as well as in the coaching process; and provide insight into, an appreciation of, and respect for different styles and information-processing abilities.

4. *Provide time for people to experiment.* Since experimentation is a key norm, time needs to be allocated for participants to experiment and then come together to solve problems and relate their experiences with applying the training.

5. *Hold review and refinement sessions.* These "R and R" sessions offer peer coaches an opportunity to perfect existing skills and refine coaching practices. In the process, much sharing and problem solving goes on, contributing to collegiality.

6. *Allocate time for support groups and study groups to meet.* Support groups provide a structure through which difficult issues can be addressed and teachers can teach one another. Often, as a result of action research or coaching interactions, teachers want to pursue a particular course of study. Study groups provide a forum for doing so.

7. *Monitor implementation activities and make adjustments as necessary.* The benchmarks of progress developed during vision building should be revisited

regularly to determine the need for any adjustments. Expect that some peer coaching activities might not fit within your school context and may need to be altered. Encourage staff feedback about implementation efforts.

8. *Provide a public forum for celebrations of peer coaching successes.* Research shows that, halfway through a change effort, a condition known as *entropy* commonly sets in. The change process loses momentum during this period. To counteract entropy, celebrations should be held to recognize successes, review the history of the effort, note progress, and energize the parties involved in the coaching effort. These celebrations might occur during a faculty meeting (at the beginning of the agenda, not the end!), at board meetings, or at special events such as a faculty brunch. Some schools use local media to celebrate positive teacher initiatives.

Institutionalization

Ultimately, peer coaching should become a part of the school culture; it becomes "the way we do things around here." In this state, it is no longer an innovation but an integral part of the institution itself. To achieve this status, the organization's members must perceive peer coaching activities as meaningful, useful, and worth continuing. The processes must become embedded in the way school business is conducted: how the school solves problems, shares in decision making, and applauds individual initiatives. Institutionalization is, perhaps, the most difficult of the three phases to accomplish. To help maintain the momentum for peer coaching:

1. *Continue the celebrations.* Create special events that celebrate peer coaching accomplishments on an ongoing basis. One school holds a brunch where teachers share stories, acknowledge one another's successes, and plan for next year. A byproduct of these events is that teachers gain a sense of efficacy. People will continue practices that they find personally meaningful and useful.

2. *Support teachers as researchers.* Build in planning time, allocate resources, and provide opportunities to

network so that, as reflective practitioners, teachers continue to grow.

3. *Continue administrative support.* Administrators and other school leaders can use several tools to focus attention, convey importance, influence attitudes, and reinforce values toward peer coaching:

- Allocating financial resources for peer coaching
- Modeling risk taking and experimentation
- Spending time on and paying attention to peer coaching in meetings
- Asking questions about peer coaching
- Conducting peer coaching sessions in special settings to convey its importance
- Placing peer coaching information in memos, newsletters, daily bulletins, and reports
- Telling stories and using metaphors to underscore the importance of peer coaching
- Structuring the decision-making and problem-solving processes used in meetings to reflect peer coaching practices
- Placing peer coaching items at the top of faculty meeting agendas
- Developing slogans or a logo to keep peer coaching in the forefront of school life.

4. *Provide brush-up sessions.* Review skills taught during the initial training sessions so that they can be refined and perfected. Some teachers work extensively, for example, on observation and conferencing skills.

5. *Continue to monitor.* Determine to what extent goals have been met and what adjustments are needed. Look for evidence that peer coaching practices are being institutionalized. Be aware that subtle evidence also exists. For instance, do faculty discussions focus on how teachers teach and students learn? Recognize, when differences surface, that "shared governance gives everyone equal rights and responsibilities to influence schoolwide decisions, and it intensifies ideological debate" (Glickman 1990).

6. *Allocate rewards.* Provide public and private recognition for accomplishments. Many rewards will surface automatically as a result of peer coaching becoming institutionalized. For example, at one school, parents noted,

"What a together staff! They are really good at problem solving." Another school, previously considered "one of the most difficult places to work" because of its inner-city population, is now one of the most desirable places to work.

7. *Invite teachers to reflect on and write about their peer coaching activities.* Teachers can add to the knowledge base about coaching by composing articles for professional journals and keeping records of their coaching experiences. These written accounts spread the good word to other professionals and provide intrinsic rewards and professional growth opportunities for teachers.

Miles and Louis (1987) offer the following "signposts of success" as indicators of institutionalization:

• The change is accepted by relevant actors.

• Implementation is stable and routine.

• The change is widely used.

• Continuation is expected and usually accompanied by negotiated agreements.

• The change has achieved legitimacy and normality; it is no longer seen as a change but has become invisible and is taken for granted.

• The change is person-independent; continuation does not depend on the actions of specific individuals, but on organizational structure, procedures, or culture.

• Allocations of time and money are routinely made.

When peer coaching becomes a real part of school operations, schools maximize their capacity to meet the challenges of today's world. Teachers are empowered to make decisions about their work, the restructured workplace, and their students. They feel responsible for the program's success. Coaching no longer is a superficial innovation tacked onto the school for a year; rather, it is part of the school's inner workings, its soul—deep and enduring. When peer coaching is institutionalized, teachers' lives change. As one teacher remarked, "Even for the most severe problems, there is colleagueship and, beyond that, companionship. The support is limitless. I don't feel alone anymore."

APPENDIX
ASCD Resources for Peer Coaching

The following resources represent products that can be used to implement a peer coaching program.

Product	Use
Changing School Culture Through Staff Development 1990 ASCD Yearbook	Provides an understanding of how peer coaching needs to become part of the institution, along with insights about collegiality, school culture, the collegial workplace, and the restructured school.
Readings from Educational Leadership: Coaching and Staff Development	Articles about coaching and staff development that can be used in program planning and awareness building.
Opening Doors: An Introduction to Peer Coaching An ASCD videotape	Can be used for orienting staff to peer coaching. Provides examples of mirroring, collaborative, and expert conferences.
Another Set of Eyes: Conferencing Skills An ASCD videotape series	Demonstrates the cognitive coaching approach and models critical communication skills.
Another Set of Eyes: Observation Skills An ASCD videotape series	Introduces a variety of data collection techniques.

Assisting Change in Education
(Trainer's Manual), by Saxl, Miles,
and Lieberman

A useful guide for
facilitators; includes specific
guidelines for implementing
the change process.

For additional information, call ASCD at 703-578-9600 or
1-800-933-2723 (press 2 for customer service).

References

Barth, R. (1990). *Improving Schools from Within*. San Francisco: Jossey-Bass, Inc.

Berliner, D. (1984). "The Half-Full Glass: A Review of the Research on Teaching." In *Using What We Know About Teaching*, edited by P.L. Hosford. Alexandria, Va.: Association for Supervision and Curriculum Development.

Berman, P., and M. McLaughlin. (1978). *Federal Programs Supporting Educational Change: Vol. VIII. Implementing and Sustaining Innovations*. Santa Monica, Calif.: The Rand Corporation.

Bird, T. (1985). Address delivered at a retreat for mentor teachers. Napa, Calif.

Caro, D., and P. Robbins. (November 1991). "Talk Walking: Thinking On Your Feet. A Strategy for Professional Enrichment, Experience and Exercise." *The Developer*, in press.

Costa, A., and R. Garmston. (1990). *The Art of Cognitive Coaching: Supervision for Intelligent Teaching* (Training Syllabus). Sacramento, Calif.: Institute for Intelligent Behavior.

Deal, T., and A. Kennedy. (1982). *Corporate Cultures*. Reading, Mass.: Addison-Wesley Publishing Co., Inc.

Flinders, D. (Fall 1988) "Teacher Isolation and the New Reform." *Journal of Curriculum and Supervision* 4, 1: 17-29.

Fullan, M. (1982). *The Meaning of Education Change*. New York: Teachers College Press.

Fullan, M. (1990). "Staff Development, Innovation, and Institutional Development." In *Changing School Culture Through Staff Development*, edited by B. Joyce.

Alexandria, Va.: Association for Supervision and Curriculum Development.

Fullan, M., B. Bennett, and C. Rolheiser-Bennett. (1989). "Linking Classroom and School Improvement." Paper presented at the annual meeting of the American Educational Research Association, San Francisco.

Fullan, M., and A. Pomfret. (1977). "Research on Curriculum and Instruction Implementation." *Review of Educational Research* 5, 47: 335-397.

Garmston, R. (February 1987). "How Administrators Support Peer Coaching." *Educational Leadership* 44, 50: 18-28.

Glatthorn, A. (1984). *Differentiated Supervision.* Alexandria, Va.: Association for Supervision and Curriculum Development.

Glickman, C. (September 1990). "Pushing School Reform to a New Edge: The Seven Ironies of School Empowerment." *Phi Delta Kappan 72, 1: 68-72.*

Gregorc, A. (1985). *Inside Styles Beyond the Basics.* Maynard, Mass.: Gabriel Systems, Inc.

Hall, G., and S. Hord. (1987). *Change in Schools: Facilitating the Process.* Albany: State University of New York Press.

Hargreaves, A. (1989). "Teacher Development and Teachers' Work: Issues of Time and Control." Paper presented at the International Conference on Teacher Development, Toronto.

Jackson, P. (1968). *Life in Classrooms.* New York: Holt, Rinehart, and Winston.

Joyce, B., and B. Showers. (February 1980). "Improving Inservice Training: The Messages of Research." *Educational Leadership* 37, 5: 379-385.

Lieberman, A., and L. Miller. (April 1981). "Synthesis of Research on Improving Schools." *Educational Leadership* 38, 7: 583-586.

Little, J. W. (1981). *School Success and Staff Development: The Role of Staff Development in Urban Desegregated Schools, Executive Summary.* Washington, D.C.: National Institute of Education.

Little, J. W. (1982). "Norms of Collegiality and Experimentation: Workplace Conditions of School

Success." *American Educational Research Journal* 19, 3: 325-340.

Little, J. W. (1985a). Address delivered at a retreat for mentor teachers, Napa, Calif.

Little, J. W. (November 1985b). "Teachers as Teacher Advisers: The Delicacy of Collegial Leadership." *Educational Leadership* 43: 34-36.

Little, J. W. (1989). "The 'Mentor' Phenomenon and the Social Organization of Teaching." *Review of Research in Education* 5, 16. Washington, D.C.: American Educational Research Association.

Mid-Continent Regional Educational Laboratory. (1983). *Coaching: A Powerful Strategy in Improving Staff Development and Inservice Education.* Kansas City: Mid-Continent Regional Educational Laboratory.

Miles, M., and K. Louis. (1987). "Research on Institutionalization: A Reflective Review." In *Lasting School Improvement: Exploring the Process of Institutionalization.* Leuven, Belgium: OECD.

Robbins, P. (1984). *The Napa-Vacaville Follow Through Research Project.* (Final Report). Washington, D.C.: National Institute of Education.

Roberts, L., et al. (December 1987). *Helping Your Staff Grow Professionally* (Training Manual). Hayward: California School Leadership Academy.

Rosenholtz, S. (1989). *Teachers' Workplace.* New York: Longman.

Saxl, E., M. Miles, and A. Lieberman. (1989). *Assisting Change in Education* (Trainer's Manual). New York: Center for Policy Research; Seattle: University of Washington; and Alexandria, Va.: Association for Supervision and Curriculum Development.

Seller, W., and L. Hannay. (1988). "The Influence of School Climate on Peer Coaching." Paper presented at the annual meeting of the American Educational Research Association, New Orleans.

Shulman, L. (1991). Address presented at the Annual Conference of the Association for Supervision and Curriculum Development, San Francisco.

Sizer, T. (1985). *Horace's Compromise: The Dilemma of the American High School.* Boston: Houghton-Mifflin Co.

Sparks, G. M. (November 1983). "Synthesis of Research on Staff Development for Effective Teaching." *Educational Leadership* 41, 3: 65-72.

Stallings, J., and G. Mohlman. (1981). *School Policy, Leadership Style, Teacher Change, and Student Behavior in Eight Schools: Final Report.* Washington, D.C.: National Institute of Education.